A CALL TO THE FEET OF GOD
DECLARATIONS THROUGH SCRIPTURE

Trilogy Christian Publishers

A Wholly Owned Subsidary of Trinity Broadcasting Network

2442 Michelle Drive

Tustin, CA 92780

For information, address Trilogy Christian Publishing

Rights Department, 2442 Michelle Drive, Tustin, Ca 92780.

Trilogy Christian Publishing/ TBN and colophon are trademarks of Trinity Broadcasting Network.

For information about special discounts for bulk purchases, please contact Trilogy Christian Publishing.

Manufactured in the United States of America

10 9 8 7 6 5 4 3 2 1

Library of Congress Cataloging-in-Publication Data is available.

ISBN 978-1-63769-282-0

ISBN 978-1-63769-283-7 (ebook)

Dedications

To my husband Orsbie "Stick." You and I trusted God. And you and I were exactly what each other needed to bring out the best in each other. We are the perfect union, and our daily prayers and scripture reading has really grounded our relationship. Thank you for choosing me. I will always be your CillaB. I love you.

To Ivory, my son. I love your intelligence, your straight forwardness. A born leader, you were meant to be the oldest. Never stop being you, it is a suit-tailored to fit. I am honored to call you my son.

To Fronshua, my son. I love your eagerness, "your go-get-it" attitude. Know that God is with you and always has been. You are positioned for greater things, always look beyond your perception. I am so blessed to have you.

To Yulinseya, my only daughter. I love the way you do what you say, your determination is an inspiration and part of what makes you a great wife and mom. Everything you want is in your path. You are worthy of greatness and I am proud of you, my beauty.

To Cedric, moma's baby! You are awesome and you know it. Confidence looks good on you. You always find the good in people and the best in situations. May God continue to guide your heart. You are a treasure of love. The world is yours.

Inspirations

Mom and Pop Garrett, thank you for being my earthly parents, you both are awesome! Full of energy and life. No matter the ups and downs, your bond is something to aspire to. I love you both.

Apostle and Pastor First Lady Sibley Sr, thank you for being God's trustworthy vessels. Prophesying and loving into my life. I have watched you both feed into many lives over the years and I want to thank you for being there. I learn so much from the both of you.

Brother Kalvin and Sister Charlene Douglas, I love to see you all praise and worship God and teach His word. You both are such great role models for your girls and many of us. Keep the fire of God you both were created to motivate and inspire others.

Prologue

Discovering who I am took a long time. To get from there to now; that I am confident in who I am, I find out it is not who I am at all. I became comfortable in my identity knowing my strength and hiding my weakness. Being renewed in Christ and transformed, I found out who I discovered I was, was still not who I really am. I had to die to realize who God created me to be. Not only was I inside, but I was also in denial. I fought for a long time to find out who I was, to find out where I belong. I could not because I had yet to discover the love of God and that He has purpose for me. Dying to self has been one of the most difficult things I had to face, my flesh fought with the pulling of teeth. My mine rebelled and refused to bend. I read scripture after scripture thinking I could find a reason just to hang on to the me I thought I was. As I let some of me go, I noticed the blessings God was bestowing upon me. It inspired me to let even more of me go. Then I heard the still small voice say, "Why so many stipulations for you to be stimulated." I cried that day because I realized I was becoming vain to receive more blessings.

When the reality of it was to follow His word and He would always supply my needs. I did not want much just for the people around to be more at peace. With so much tribulation, I spent nights tossing and turning. I began to pray more and now believing, that God provides. Full nights of rest brought upon tears of joy; testimonies became my new reality. When I started doing declarations at church it brought me to the feet of God, which is His word, His son Jesus Christ. So, I will continue to search for His wisdom and the understanding thereof. God's word is so pertinent in every aspect of our lives. God said, "Behold I stand at the door and knock: if any man hear my voice, and open the door I will come in to him."

Notes....

1

I HAVE FAITH

Stone rolled away, He called death to life, spit and dirt He opened blind eyes, reached out His hand and said be though clean, He said rise take up your bed and walk. In the book of Mark 4:37-40, KJV, it tells us of Jesus and His disciples in a ship, Jesus was asleep there came a storm of wind and the waves beat upon the ship till it was full, the disciples awoke Jesus saying, "Master carest thou not that we perish?" Jesus rebuked the wind said to the sea peace be still and he said to his disciples why are you so fearful how is it that ye have no faith?

I declare grace, the unmerited love and favor of God, I have faith

I declare I am assured in things I hope for because I am convicted by the Holy Spirit, I have faith.

I declare through the sacrifice of Jesus I am reconciled with God, I have faith..

I declare I submit to the will of God where all things are possible, I have faith..

I declare healing and prosperity, peace and love joy and strength, sanctification, and deliverance I have faith.

In the mighty name of Jesus, this is my declaration.

Notes....

2
CHOOSE GOD

Formed in a womb so perfect, saved from sin before we knew we were born into sin, forgiven before we knew wrong was wrong, healed by the stripes of His Son before we felt the pain. And still He patiently waited for us to choose Him. For He is a triune God, Father, Son, and Holy Spirit. And yes, we are blessed because of it.

Today I stand in declaration that I have chosen God as the master of my life. He is my Lord.

I declare that I love Him because He first loved me.

I declare that all things are possible to me because I believe.

I declare that I worship Him in spirit and in truth.

I declare that God is with me wherever I go, God is my peace.

I declare that my life is aligned with his word and I walk in obedience to it, I am prosperous I command blessings to rain down upon me. Blessings I call you to manifest even in the lives of my friend and my foe.

I give release of me that I was, for God to use me so that His word and His will dominate this earth in the name of Jesus, this is my declaration.

Notes....

3
SIN NO MORE

Open doors are setting minds free, chains are broken from hearts with the love of peace. The will of God reigns forever more. With glory be to His son our Savior. Released from the bondage of distraction I am no longer bound to procrastination. For I have been before the throne of grace and God has granted His mercy. My faith and gratitude are in his son Jesus who has truly paved the way. Micah 7:19, KJV, says, reverencing our gracious wonderful loving Father God in Heaven who has compassion upon us, subdues our iniquities and cast our sins into the depths of the sea.

I declare to exercise self-control, to be worthy of respect.

I declare everything I do reflect integrity and seriousness of truth.

I declare to walk cautiously not as a fool but wise
because the days are evil.

I declare to be discipline in my vision for the purpose of godliness.

I declare to hold fast the confession of my hope without wavering free from a guilty conscience and washed with the pure water for he who promised is faithful.

I declare where my hope abounds joy and peace live. Steadfast in faith completely humble and gentle bearing with one another in love.

In the name of Jesus Christ, this is my declaration.

Notes....

4
STAY READY FOR WAR

No matter what we see going on, we need to understand and to know that we are in a spiritual warfare. And our belief in the finished work of Jesus Christ tells us in Ephesians 6, that we battle not against flesh and blood but against principalities, against power's, against spiritual wickedness in high places. Therefore, we must be clothed in the full armor of God. Because when an enemy sees a weakness in our armor that is when the enemy strikes.

I declare that my loins are girt about with truth,

I have on the breast plate of righteousness.

My feet are shod with the preparation of the gospel of peace.

Above all I have the shield of faith

Helmet of salvation and the sword of the spirit which is God's word.

Praying always with prayer and supplication in the spirit.

Isaiah 61:10 (KJV) I will greatly rejoice in the Lord, my soul shall be joyful in my God; for He hath clothed me with the garments of salvation, he hath covered me with the robe of righteousness, as a bridegroom decketh himself with ornaments, and as a bride adorneth herself with her jewels.

In the name of our Lord and Savior Jesus Christ,
this is my declaration!

Notes....

5

PRAISE HIM

I bow my head when I pray to Him, I lift my hands surrendering to Him, I bend my knees in respect of Him, I lie flat on my face to honor His presence. God, who will make a way out of no way. God, who supplies all our needs according to His riches in glory in Christ Jesus.

I declare that God is my strength, my peace in the storm, my light in the darkness,

My burden bearer, my way maker, my rock, my provider, my refuge, my all and all, my thank you!

My hallelujah! My Yes Lord! My Jesus! My Master!

And I declare His word is the way the truth and the life.

In the name of God, the Father, the Son, and the Holy Spirit, this is my declaration!

Notes....

6
DO YOU BELIEVE?

Holy, Holy, Holy, Lord God Almighty, which was, and is, and is to come. If you are truly blessed because you know in your heart that the promises of God are yes and Amen, then say Hallelujah!!! When you woke this morning, you picked up your cross because you knew you were following Jesus, say Amen!

I declare that I am God's workmanship, created in Christ Jesus unto good works. (Ephesians 2:10, KJV)

I declare that I do not fight for victory, I stand in the glory of the victory in Jesus.

I declare that I have been established, anointed, and sealed by God in Christ.

I declare that sin does not have dominion over me, for I am seated not under the law but under grace. (Romans 6:14, KJV)

I declare that I endure because I am committed and confident in God.

In the name of the Almighty Son, Jesus Christ, this is my declaration.

Notes....

7

CONTINUE TO CLIMB

It is time that we stand firmly in a continued state of elevation. Always ready, always Willing to answer His call. We must continue to press toward the mark of our higher calling. Fasting and praying often and quieting our minds and listening to God's direction and be led by the Holy Spirit.

I declare that I will continually seek His face.

I declare that I will never stop the hunger or the thirst for righteousness. (Matthew 5:6, KJV)

I declare to sanctify the Lord God in my heart and to always be ready to give every man an answer for my reason of hope with meekness and fear. (1 Peter 3:15, KJV)

I declare to forget those things which are behind me and reach forth to those things which are before me. (Philippians 3:13, KJV)

I declare that mountains moved, enemies defeated, because I stand in Christ Jesus.

In the name of God, the Father, the Son, and the Holy Spirit, this is my declaration.

Notes....

8
BECAUSE HE IS

All praises to our good and compassionate God and Father, in the name of His Son Jesus who overcame the world. And with our faith in when Jesus said, "it is finished" (John 19:30 KJV) many blessings are made available. We have divine intercession and can go before God in Jesus wonderful name. We can speak God's Word out loud and boldly into existence with the no faith, that is the confidence and the assurance that it is so.

I declare that I stand in God given authority.

I declare increased vision due to my increased faith.

I declare I look beyond circumstances because restoration and progression have begun.

I declare I look forward to God daily blessing me, for eyes have not seen nor ears heard all God has for me.

I am a prosperous disciple, in the name of God the father, the Son, and the Holy Spirit, this is my declaration.

Notes....

9
HE IN ME

For I cry not for yesterday, but for today. For the hope of God's people. That they love one another as God love's each one all the same. I cry for the unity of the people that we become one, one focus, one God, the one true God in Heaven. I cry for no more hunger, homeless or despair. Though He did not say there would not be tribulation, He did say that he has plans that we may prosper and not to harm, a hope and a future. I cry the light of God shines upon us all, that we stand in His glory as His fiery wall of protection surrounds us all. I cry for the sacrifice that brought us grace and mercy.

I declare my refuge and my fortress my God in whom I trust.

I declare that I am anxious for nothing for God is with me.

I declare that even though the enemy come upon me they will
stumble and fall, for greater is He that is within me,
than he that is in the world.

I declare so a man thinketh in his heart so is he, therefore, my heart
thinketh I am rich in charity and of wealth, so I am.

In the name of Jesus Christ , this is my declaration.

Notes....

10

LET GOD BE THE GUIDE

God loads us daily with benefits and our perfect peace comes from the peace of God which passeth all understanding. Which keeps our hearts and minds through Christ, who said, "My peace I leave with you, my peace I give unto you, not as the world giveth, give I unto thee. Let not your heart be troubled neither let it be afraid." (Psalms 68:19; Philippians 4:7; John 14:1, 27, KJV)

I declare that I surrender the me that I know,
so that His will for my life to be done.

I declare that I will trust in the guidance of His holy spirit.

I declare that I will delight myself in the excellence of the Lord.

I declare I will seek Him daily through prayer and scripture.

I declare that I will rest always in his peace.

In the name of our Lord and Savior Jesus Christ,
this is my declaration.

Notes....

11

WHO I AM

It is time that we remind ourselves of who God says we are; because so often things are left incomplete because we lose ourselves when we forget who we are. You see, who God says we are gives us power and our belief in and because of His son Jesus, that, gives us authority. Psalms 139:17-18 (KJV) How precious also are thy thoughts of me, O God! How great is the sum of them! If I could count them, they are more than the sum of the sand. When I awake, I am still with thee.

I declare I am who God says I am, Blessed, loved, worthy, powerful,

anointed, redeemed, gifted, chosen, favored, victorious, a masterpiece, bold,

wanted, protected, beautiful, wondrously made

set apart and set free, I am His!

I declare I am who God says I am.

In the name of God, the Father, the Son, and the Holy Spirit, this is my declaration.

Notes....

12

MY ASSIGNMENT

Blessings are being manifested, prayers answered, eyes are opening, and ears are listening. Tell them to seek God's counsel through His word. As kingdom builders, we must continue to grow in God, with a determined heart and mind that abides in the vine.

I declare that nothing is more important than what God has me here to do.

I declare that I am a kingdom builder, an atmosphere shifter (Matthew 28:18-20)

I declare to rejoice evermore, pray without ceasing praise him in all things. (1 Thessalonians 5:16-17)

I declare though much tribulation I will continue in faith (Acts 14:22)

By the power of His name, our Lord and Savior Jesus Christ, this is my declaration.

Notes....

13
HOPE

My fellow believers, when it seems as though you are facing nothing but difficulties, see it as an invaluable opportunity to experience the greatest joy you can. For you know that when your faith is tested it stirs up a power within you to endure all things. And then, as your endurance grows even stronger, it will release perfection into every part of your being until there is nothing missing or nothing lacking. (James 1:2-4, TPT)

I declare that I am energized with God's explosive power from His magnificent glory, filling me with great hope. (Colossians 1:11, TPT)

I declare God is my inspiration and fountain of hope, He fills me with uncontainable joy and perfect peace as I trust in Him. (Romans 15:13, TPT)

I declare to stay alert and hold firm to all that I believe, being mighty and full of courage. (1 Corinthians 16:13, TPT)

I declare I will run life's marathon race with passion and determination for the path has already been marked before me. (Hebrews 12:1, TPT)

I declare this is all achieved with my obedience to His word.

In the name of my Lord and Savior - Jesus Christ, this is my declaration.

Notes....

14

PROVIDER

Trials are troubling, but God delivers. Heart's break, but God heals; danger all around, but God is a protector. The money seems never enough, until you trust God and He multiplies. Love one another and live for God. For your belief in the finish works of His Son awakens your faith and will ignite your confidence and assurance that God provides.

I declare to be cheerful with joyous celebration in every season of life. (Philippians 4:4, TPT)

I declare to being one body and one spirit as I was called in the same glorious hope of divine destiny. (Ephesians 4:4, TPT)

I declare blessings of divine grace and supernatural peace from God. (Philippians 1:2, TPT)

I declare I speak those things that be not as though they were. (Romans 4:17, KJV)

I declare God has favor upon my life I awake in expectation and

I go to sleep in thanksgiving.

I stand in the grace of Him who died for me.

I am blessed by God because of Jesus and this is my declaration.

Notes....

15
JESUS

Our Lord and Savior walked the Earth and taught the word to all who would listen, healed the sick and raised the dead. Along the way He said, "I am the way." He said, "I am the bread of life, I am the light of the world, I am the door, I am the good shepherd, I am the resurrection, the way the truth and the life, I am the vine. No one comes to my Father except by Me." His name is Jesus!

I declare He hung up on a cross until He said it is finished.
He is my sacrifice. (John 19:30, KJV)

I declare I follow Jesus He guides my feet into the way of peace.
He is my light. (Luke 1:79, KJV)

I declare for the grace given unto me. I will not think
more highly of myself than I ought.

He is my grace. (Romans 12:3, KJV)

I declare Jesus stands at the right hand of God. He is my savior.
(Acts 7:55, KJV)

I declare to humble myself in the sight of the Lord so he shall
lift me up. He is my strength. (James 4:10, KJV)

I declare the name above all names every knee in heaven and on
earth shall bow and every tongue confess Jesus Christ is Lord.
(Philippians 2:10, KJV)

To the glory of God, the Father, and in His powerful name,
this is my declaration.

Notes....

16
BECAUSE OF HIM

With all glory and honor given to our creator God in Heaven. In the name of His Son who came by the spirit unto a virgin to be raised by a carpenter, and then baptized by one who was crying in the wilderness, as heaven opened and the spirit of God descended upon Him as a dove, then to hear the voice of God from heaven say this is my son in whom I am well pleased. Then led by the Spirit where for forty days He defeated the enemy by the words of His Father our God.

I declare every good work is because of God's abounding grace.
(2 Corinthians 9:8, KJV)

I declare because of the Lord's mercy we are not consumed because his compassion fail not. (Lamentation 3:22, KJV)

I declare the Lord is my portion saith my soul therefore I will hope in Him. (Lamentation 3:24, KJV)

I declare the fruit of my lips give thanks to His name.
(Hebrews 13:15, KJV)

I declare the work of God because I believe in Him who He sent.
(John 6:29, KJV)

In the name and love of Jesus Christ with all sincerity,
this is my declaration.

Notes....

UNLIKE YOU OR ME

How could one think more highly of himself than he ought? When there is no way that you or I would give of oneself for the fate of a world, a world filled with disobedience and ungratefulness. On the hope that this world just might believe or better yet completely submit themselves in the hope of an unseen God!

I declare recognition of Jesus Christ is the son of the living God: and His teaching is the foundation of my life.
(Matthew 16:16, KJV)

I declare selflessness, denying myself and taking up my cross and following Jesus. (Matthew 16:24, KJV)

I declare humility as I wash the feet of my brother as my Master and Lord did to His disciples. (John 13:14, KJV)

I declare devotion to His word as I shall be there when the Son of Man returns in the glory of His father with angels about Him.
(Matthew 16:27, KJV)

For the sacrificial lamb, my Lord and Savior Jesus Christ, this is my declaration.

Notes....

18

THE FRUIT

The fruit of the Holy Spirit within you is divine love in all its varied expressions. Joy that overflows, Peace that subdues. Longsuffering that is kindness in action. Gentleness of heart. Goodness that is a life full of virtue, faith that prevails, meekness that is being humble, and temperance the strength of spirit. There is no law against these qualities, for they are meant to be limitless. Galatians 5:22-23 (TPT, KJV)

I declare to know the width and length and depth and height of the love of Christ with all the fullness of God. (Ephesians 3:9, KJV)

I declare in the midst of everything, I give thanks because I continue to feast on joy because Christ life is within me.
(1 Thessalonians 5:16-18, TPT)

I declare the Lord of peace Himself give me peace always by all means and be with me. (2 Thessalonians 3:16, KJV)

I declare that I endeavor to keep the unity of the Spirit in the bond of peace. (Ephesians 2:22, KJV)

I declare these virtues are deep within me in abundance, and they keep me from being fruitless.

Galatians 5:25 (KJV) says, to live in the spirit, I must also walk in the spirit.

May grace and peace be multiplied onto me through the knowledge of God and of Jesus our Lord.

This is my declaration.

Notes....

19
I IN HIM

He is the light in our eyes, the blood flowing through our veins, the beat of our heart, the tilt in our neck, the movement in our bodies the desire of our soul, even that warm fuzzy feeling to let us know that we are not alone. Romans 8:38-39 (KJV) says, "For I am persuaded that neither death, nor life, nor angels, nor principalities, nor powers, nor things present, nor things to come, nor height, nor depth, nor any other creature shall be able to separate us from the Love of God who is in Christ Jesus our Lord.

I declare God is my author, founder, creator, and publisher,
I am established in Him through Christ Jesus.

I declare I will take surprisingly bold risk to
complete the purpose He placed in me.

I declare because God is love, He gave me Jesus,
being selfless, sacrificial, and unconditional.

I declare God's love for me deserves me to be a warrior
in His word for His will His way.

I declare God sustains me, that is physically,
mentally, and financially.

In He who gave His word, and in the word that became man, Jesus,
this is my declaration.

Notes....

20
GRACE

We do not deserve it, but it is the free unmerited favor of God. It is GRACE. Philippians 2:13, (KJV) For it is God who works in you to will and to do of His good pleasure.

I declare to live my life empowered by God's free flowing grace.

I declare to be gentle with all meekness, instructing those that oppose to see the truth.

I declare by the grace of God, I am what I am,
and His grace is not in vain.

I declare thew grace of God allows me to live a self-controlled, upright, and godly life, awaiting my blessed hope for the appearance of the great God and our Savior Jesus Christ.

I declare God show His exceeding riches of His grace in His kindness toward us through Christ Jesus.

For the salvation and blessing bestowed upon a sinner like me, I thank God for grace through our Lord and Savior Jesus Christ.

This is my declaration.

Notes....

21

HIS MERCY

God, through His mercy, not only sent His son to give us a way into His eternal life; but in doing so He made it possible for us to become one with His only begotten son. To be baptized, that is not only demonstrate our obedience in His word, but also that we repent and ask forgiveness of our sins and through our faith in Jesus, absolution – we are forgiven and released of the shame we feel.

I declare that we pray continually, that we fall not into temptation.

I declare iniquities released and true freedom rejoice.

I declare that access of the enemy to our thoughts be denied and God's word be increased.

I declare that the boundaries we place on God be removed.

I declare that we allow the spiritual gifts on the inside to come front and center.

Jesus said in John 14, that "whatsoever you ask in my name, that will I do, so that the Father may be glorified in the Son."

In the name of Jesus Christ, this is my declaration.

Notes....

22

FORGIVE YOUR ENEMY

When one comes and their tongue is further from the east to the west, and they walk a line that comforts only themselves; we are to show them the grace given to us by our Lord. When one come with steam bellowing, begin to praise God because you are covered by the blood.

I declare that the unmerited favor God have on my life be used to give my brethren a helping hand.

I declare that because the forgiveness I have been given that I am able to forgive my enemy.

I declare that I am a servant of God
for the edification of His church.

I declare that I am blessed to be a blessing. For I am blessed in the city and blessed going out.

Psalms 91:2, KJV says, The Lord is my refuge and my fortress, my God; in Him will I trust.

In the name of our Lord and Savior Jesus Christ
this is my declaration.

Notes....

23
UNLIMITED GOODNESS

Almighty God in heaven is unlimited in His goodness and because of His goodness, everything that we shall ever need is in the power of the name of His son Jesus. If we are to seek wisdom, peace, wealth, riches, and as a bonus, everlasting life. We must submit ourselves to His word and His way in the name of Jesus. And all those blessing will be given unto us. In 1 Corinthians 1:20 (KJV) says that the promises of God in Him is yea and amen.

I declare the word of Jesus never to go hungry because He is my
bread and never to be thirsty because I believe in Him.
(John 6:35, KJV)

I declare the thoughts that the Lord has of me are of peace and not
of evil and to give me an expected end. (Jeremiah 29:11, KJV)

I declare to give, and it shall be given unto me; good measure, press
down and shaken together shall men give unto me.
(Luke 6:38, KJV)

I declare because of my love for God, He says that eye hath not seen
nor ear heard neither have entered the heart of man, all the things
God hath prepared for me. (1 Corinthians 2:9, KJV)

I declare the grace of our Lord Jesus Christ, that though He was rich
became poor for our sakes, that through his poverty we might be
rich. (2 Corinthians 8:9, KJV)

By the agape love of our creator, in Jesus's name,
this is my declaration

Notes....

24

FEARFUL YET STRONG

Throughout the Bible, there are great stories of everyday people who became strong in God. They were faithful to His word, they were fearful of His wrath, and determined to be what He needed them to be. They achieved what they set out to do according to His commandments. Being strong minded and strong willed. In KJV of Philippians 4:13 it says I can do all things through Christ which strengthens me.

I declare that I have the determination of Nehemiah.

I declare that I have the obedience of Noah.

I declare that I am chosen like Moses.

I declare that I have the foresight in prophecy of Isaiah.

I declare that I have the wisdom of Solomon.

I declare that I will stand for God like Job.

I declare that I will dance like David danced, because that's just how good God is to me.

In the name of His son Jesus Christ, this is my declaration.

Notes....

25
CLEANSED

Come now, and let us reason together says the Lord, though your sins are like scarlet they shall be as white as snow; Though they are red like crimson, they shall be as wool. If you are willing and obedient you shall eat the good of the land. (Isaiah 1:18-19, KJV)

I declare to forgive others so that my heavenly Father will forgive me. (Matthew 6:14, KJV)

I declare to confess and forsake my sins so that I may receive mercy. (Proverbs 28:13, KJV)

I declare redemption through His blood, the forgiveness of sins according with the riches of God's grace. (Ephesians 1:7, KJV)

I declare to forget those things which are behind me and reach forward to those things which are ahead. (Philippians 3:13, KJV)

I declare the Lord to show compassion on us and to tread our iniquities underfoot and cast all our sins into the depths of the sea. (Micah 7:19, KJV)

All hope in our Lord and Savior who bared the cross and once again wears His crown Jesus Christ, this is my declaration.

Notes....

26

THE CROSS

Looking unto Jesus, the author and finisher of our faith, who for the joy that was set before Him endured the cross, despising the shame and has sat down at the right hand of the throne of God. For consider Him who endured such hostility from sinners against Himself, lest ye become weary and discouraged in your souls. (Hebrews 12:2-3, NKJV)

I declare that because of Jesus upon the cross, gift of the Holy Spirit.

I declare that because of Jesus upon the cross,
God gives to the believer, grace, and mercy.

I declare that because of Jesus upon the cross,
we are redeemed from the curse of the law.

I declare that because of Jesus upon the cross,
there is opportunity for remission of sin.

I declare that because of Jesus upon the cross,
the availability of salvation.

I declare that because of Jesus upon the cross
I have the chance of life everlasting.

In the name of the scourged, crucified, and risen Jesus Christ
my Savior, this is my declaration.

Notes....

27
GOD MULTIPLIES

Once He fed five thousand people with two fish and five loaves. Then He fed the multitude with seven loaves and a few fish. The multitude was of four thousand men and besides the men there were also women and children. His disciples learned during these days to trust Jesus for yet with only a little faith in God, He multiplies. There were even baskets left over. Jesus knew who He was and the power He possessed and of what He as the Son of God would say, and His Father would do.

I declare my soul is anchored in hope, both sure and steadfast which enters the presence behind the veil. (Hebrews 6:19, KJV)

I declare hope maketh not ashamed because the love of God is shed abroad in our hearts by the Holy Ghost which is given unto us. (Romans 5:5, KJV)

I declare blessed be the God and Father of Jesus Christ, the living hope through the resurrection of Jesus from the dead. (1 Peter 1:3, KJV)

I declare to wait upon the Lord, my strength will be renewed, I will mount up with wings as eagles, I will run and not be weary, I will walk and not faint. (Isiah 40:31, KJV)

I declare I am blessed I trust in the Lord and the Lord is my hope. I am as the tree planted by the waters. (Jeremiah 17:7-8, KJV)

Blessed be the Father Son and Holy Spirit in Jesus's mighty name, this is my declaration.

Notes....

28

BE ZEALOUS

Jesus came and set an example, to turn the other cheek and make unlimited forgiveness; to love your neighbor as thyself; to set our affection on things above not of this earth and to stand still and see the salvation of the Lord.

I declare to be zealous in my faithfulness to God; by continuing in prayer and watching in the same with thanksgiving (Colossians 4:2, KJV)

I declare to walk in wisdom toward them that are without, redeeming the time (Colossians 4:5, KJV)

I declare to owe no man anything but to love one another (Romans 13:8, KJV)

I declare to be consistent in my growth as I become more and more Christ like; by pressing toward the mark of the high calling of God in Christ Jesus (Philippians 3:14, KJV)

I declare to live in the power of an endless life (Hebrews 7:16, KJV) and to do justly, to love mercy and to walk humbly with God (Micah 6:8, KJV)

Magnify Him, Glorify Him, for He is Lord, Savior and Redeemer in Jesus name, this is my declaration.

Notes....

29

GOD'S TIMING

In God's timing everything is right and perfect. The complete road we are to travel while waiting on Him is predestined. If it is Gods will, it will be achieved in His way. Psalms 37:7 TPT) Quiet your heart in His presence and pray. Keep hope alive as you long for God to come through to you. And don't think for a moment that the wicked in their prosperity are better off than you.

I declare I will look unto the Lord, I will wait for the God of my salvation and my God will hear me. (Micah 7:7, KJV)

I declare to wait for the Lord, my whole being waits, and in His word, I put my hope. My soul waits for the Lord more than they that wait for the morning to come. (Psalms 130:5-6, NIV)

I declare the Lord is good to those who wait on Him, to the soul that seeketh Him. (Lamentations 2:25, KJV)

I declare to be hoping, trusting, and waiting on the Lord, for He is tenderhearted kind and forgiving, with Him is plenteous redemption. (Psalms 130:7, KJV)

I declare regardless of my perception the Lord is not late in His promises, His longsuffering is because He does not want me to perish but to repent. (2 Peter 3:9, NIV)

I will wait on the Lord and be of good courage, He shall strengthen my heart. I will wait. (Psalms 27:14, KJV)

In the might name of Jesus, this is my declaration.

Notes....

30
LOVE

If I were to speak with eloquence in earth's many languages, and in heavenly tongues of angels, yet I did not express myself with love, my words would be reduced to the hollow sound of nothing more than a clanging cymbal. (1 Corinthians 13:1, TPT)

I declare to do everything in Love. (1 Corinthians 16:14, NIV)

I declare to love life, keep my tongue from evil, to seek peace and pursue it. (Psalms 34:14, NIV)

I declare I love Jesus and I keep His commandments. (John 14:15, KJV)

I declare to love one to another earnestly as love covers a multitude of sins. (1 Peter 4:8, NIV)

I declare greater love has no one than one who would lay down His life for His friends. (John 15:13, KJV)

1 Corinthians 13:8 (TPT) says, Love never stops loving. It extends beyond the gift of prophecy, which will eventually fade away. It is more enduring than tongues which will one day fall silent.

For God so loved the world that He gave His only begotten Son, this is my declaration of Love.

Notes....

31
HE CALL ME HIS OWN

We are all worthy of agape love from a triune God, so righteous, perfect, irreplaceable, undeniable, omniscience, omnipotent, omnipresent, and omnibenevolent. And He calls me His own.

I declare to praise Him! who is the health of my countenance and my God. (Psalms 42:11, KJV)

I declare victory in the Lord! because I am strong in the Lord and the power of his might. (Ephesians 6:10, KJV)

I declare prosperity in Him! to acquaint now thyself with Him, and be at peace, thereby good shall come unto thee. (Job 22:21, KJV)

I declare that I will serve Him with gladness and into His presence with singing. (Psalms 100:2, KJV)

I declare holding for the word of life that I may rejoice in the day of Christ that I have not run in vain, neither labored in vain. (Philippians 2:2, KJV)

With blessings, glory, wisdom, thanksgiving, honor, power and might be unto God for ever, this is my declaration.

Notes....

32

PRAY THE WORD

1 Kings 2, David said to Solomon, "I go the way of all the earth; be strong, therefore, and prove yourself a man. And keep the charge of the Lord your God; to walk in His ways, to keep His statutes, His commandments, His judgments, and His testimonies.

I declare in prayer the word of God that He must increase, and I must decrease. (John 3:30 KJV)

I declare in prayer the word of God to call upon Him and He will show me great and mighty things that I do not know. (Jeremiah 33:3, KJV)

I declare in prayer the word of God to pay attention to what I hear, the closer I listen the more I will be given, and I will receive even more. (Mark 4:24, NLT)

I declare in prayer the word of God to commit my works to the Lord, and thy thoughts shall be established. (Proverbs 16:3, KJV)

I declare in prayer the word of God to remember that It is He who gives the power to get wealth. (Deuteronomy 8:18, KJV)

Proverbs 3:5, KJV, Trust in the Lord with all thine heart and lean not unto thine own understanding.

In the mighty name of Jesus, this is my declaration.

Notes....

33
CALLED TO BE

Called to praise, to glorify Him: to worship, to give homage to Him: to serve, allow others to see Him through you: and to feed, share the good news of the gospel to all people.

I declare I am a holy partaker of a heavenly calling
(Hebrews 3:1, KJV)

I declare I was called out of darkness into his marvelous light
(1 Peter 2:9, KJV)

I declare I was called to use the gifts I received to serve others as good stewards of the manifold grace of God. (1 Peter 4:10, KJV)

I declare to present my body as a living sacrifice, holy acceptable until God as my reasonable service. (Romans 12:1, KJV)

I declare through the tender mercy of God, to give light to those that sit in darkness and in the shadow of death, to guide our feet into the way of peace. (Luke 1;78-79, KJV)

In the name of Jesus who was sent not to judge but to save, this is my declaration.

Notes....

34
LET GO AND LET GOD

The cry to the chirp, a bark or an oink, a purr or a roar, a growl or a howl, the flow of water, shine of the sun, the whisper of wind, dawn of the moon, the aroma of fresh flowers and even the dirt after the rain: take a deep breath and feel the love of God so kind and tender, whose always around. Acknowledge His works and the gift of His tongue. Just how much He loves both you and me if we just believe.

I declare to cast all my cares upon Him; He careth for me.
(1 Peter 5:7, KJV)

I declare to have faith in God. (Mark 11:22, KJV)

I declare with God nothing is impossible. (Luke 1:37, KJV)

I declare with the shield of faith I am able to quench fiery darts of
the wicked. (Ephesians 6:16, KJV)

I declare the body without a spirit is dead just as faith without
works is dead also. (James 2:26, KJV)

I am a hearer and a doer of God's word thanks be to Jesus,
this is my declaration.

Notes....

35

SEEK HIS FACE

We should evermore seek the face of our creator, His son who came that we might have life everlasting. To worship at His feet, singing psalms of praise as we bask in His presence.

I declare that I seek the Lord in all I do, and my heart rejoices in His strength. (Psalms 105:3-4, KJV)

I declare to remember His marvelous works and wonders of times past and times to come and not to forget that His judgments are in all the earth. (Psalms 105:5,7, KJV)

I declare to ask, and it shall be given, to seek so that I may find, and knock so that it may be opened. (Matthew 7:7, KJV)

I declare salvation because Jesus came to seek me for, I once was lost. (Luke 19:10, KJV)

I declare to seek the knowledge of wisdom unto my soul where there shall be a reward and my expectation shall not be cutoff (Proverbs 24:14, KJV)

I will walk in liberty as I seek His precepts, in the name of Jesus, this is my declaration.

Notes....

36

ALREADY DONE

There is nothing too big that God cannot do. Studying His word arms us with the word that is sharper than any two-edged sword; making us able to defeat the enemy with the word of the one who brought this creation into existence, with His word. 2 Samuel 22:2-3 (KJV) The Lord is my rock, and my fortress, and my deliverer; my God, my rock in Him will I trust, He is my shield and the horn of my salvation, my high tower, and my refuge, my savior; thou savest me from violence.

I declare the Lord goes with me to fight against my enemies and give me the victory. (Deuteronomy 20:4, NIV)

I declare God hath not given me the spirit of fear; but of power, and of love, and of a sound mind. (2 Timothy 1:7, KJV)

I declare the Lord is my strength and my song He has become my salvation. (Psalms 118:14, KJV)

I declare the Lord gives power to the faint and those without might He gives strength. (Isaiah 40:29, KJV)

I declare God arms me with strength and keeps my way secure. (Psalm 18:32, NIV)

All glory to the everlasting God, the Lord, the creator to the ends of the Earth.

This is my declaration.

Notes....

37

UNDERSTANDING

These things God is and has made available to us: perfection and goodness, inspiration and motivation, assurance and encouragement, freedom and truth, love and devotion, stability and dependance, and Proverbs 4:7 (KJV) says, Wisdom is the principal thing; therefore, get wisdom: and with all thy getting get understanding.

I declare the fear of the Lord is the beginning of wisdom. (Proverbs 9:10, KJV)

I declare to ask of God for wisdom, He give to all men liberally, and upbraideth not; and it shall be given him. (James 1:5, KJV)

I declare to be filled with the knowledge of God's will in all the wisdom and spiritual understanding. (Colossians 1:9, KJV)

I declare to do deeds done in humility that comes from wisdom. (James 3:13, NIV)

I declare my heart is comforted, knit together in love, unto all riches of the full assurance of understanding. (Colossians 2:2, KJV)

I declare I will not be as a fool and vent to rage. I will be wise and bring calm in the end. (Proverbs 29:11, NIV)

In the name of He who paid the price, Jesus Christ, this is my declaration.

Notes....

38

CLOSE, BUT NO HARM

Rejoice in the storm. Celebrate do not mourn. Cry for joy, not sadness. Scream hallelujah to the rooftops when you are not feeling well, decree and believe Gods word that you have already been healed. God is comfort, when you feel all is lost, He provides hope in times of despair.

I declare to forget misery and remember it as waters that pass away.
(Job 11:16, KJV)

I declare when trouble arise, I am not distressed, perplexed but not in despair, persecuted not forsaken, cast down but not destroyed.
(2 Corinthians 4:8-9, KJV)

I declare the power to tread on serpents and scorpions, and all the power of the enemy and nothing by any means shall hurt me.
(Luke 10:19, KJV)

I declare to take no thought in what I shall eat, drink or be clothed; for my heavenly Father know that I have need of these things.
(Matthew 6:31-32, KJV)

I declare the Lord is good, a stronghold in the day of trouble; and He knows who trust in Him. (Nahum 1:7, KJV)

Because thou hast made the Lord, which is my refuge, even the most High, thy habitation; there shall no evil befall thee, neither shall any plague come nigh thy dwelling. Psalms 91:9-10 (KJV)

This is my declaration.

Notes....

39
BEFORE CREATION

Bond of perfection is love. Christ is the head of the church. To live in Him means we are a bond of perfect love that knows no boundaries. Because in Him we can do all things, even love our enemies, He is our strength. Completed in Him, circumcision made without hands, buried with Him in baptism and arisen with Him through faith in the working of God Colossians 2:10-12 (KJV).

I declare that I am wrapped in the comfort of heaven and woven together into love's fabric. (Colossians 2:2, TPT)

I declare my spiritual wealth is in Christ, like hidden treasure waiting to be discovered - heaven's wisdom and endless riches of revelation knowledge. (Colossians 2:3, TPT)

I declare I am disciplined and deeply committed with solid faith in Christ. (Colossians 2:4, TPT)

I declare my spiritual roots go deeply in the life of Jesus our Lord and I am continually infused with strength and encouraged in every way. (Colossians 2:7, TPT)

I declare not to be distracted or intimidated by anyone attempting to lead me away from the fullness of Christ. (Colossians 2:7, TPT)

In the name of God who is head of every kingdom and authority in the universe, and in the name of His son Jesus Christ our Lord and Savior, this is my declaration.

Notes....

40

JUST BELIEVE

We have been fully equipped with a wealth knowledge at our fingertips, by the reading of God's word, the Bible. Receiving the knowledge to go up against what we consider our greatest adversaries; and often not recalling that the victory has already been won. Our Lord and Savior Jesus Christ has already overcome this world; it is time that we just believe.

I declare to always use the word of God, it is quick, powerful, and sharper than any two-edged sword. (Hebrews 4:12, KJV)

I declare the eyes of the Lord are in every place beholding the evil and the good. (Proverbs 15:3, KJV)

I declare to be still and know that He is God, and He will be exalted among the heathen and in the earth. (Psalms 46:10, KJV)

I declare as a servant of the Lord through whom I have righteousness it is my heritage that no weapon formed against me shall prosper. (Isiah 54:17, KJV)

I declare the Lord shall cause thine enemies that rise up against thee to be smitten, that they will come up against me one way and flee before me seven ways. (Deuteronomy 28:7, KJV)

2 Corinthians 10:4 (KJV) For the weapons of our warfare are not carnal, but mighty through God to the pulling down of strongholds.

For the power in the name of Jesus, this is my declaration.

Notes....

41
GOD

A smile upon my face, the joy that I have, my heart that flutters at the thought of His love, and the fact that He calls me His own. Revelations 4:11 (NKJV) You are worthy, O Lord, to receive glory and honor and power; for you created all things, and by your will they exist and were created.

I declare of all the things God created, He created me in His image.

I declare I am special and extraordinary.

I declare I am not average.

I declare I have been custom made.

I declare I am a light in this world.

I will keep my head held high, knowing I am a child of the Alpha and Omega, Beginning and the End, the first and the last, creator of this world and everything in it, the one and only true God, The I AM THAT I AM.

In the name of Jesus Christ, His beloved son and my Lord and Savior, this is my declaration.

Notes....

42

I WILL I AM

Be patient, generous, humble, understanding and never anxious. Eyes on God, ears open to His word, with actions on His lead. Never doubting, for without faith it is impossible to please Him; for he that cometh to God must believe that He is, and that He is a rewarder of them that diligently seek Him. Hebrews 11:6 (KJV)

I declare that I will always go to God first.

I declare that I will abide in God's word.

I declare that I will keep my mind stayed on Him and He will keep me in perfect peace.

I declare that God is my refuge and my strength.

I declare that I am thankful, grateful, and honored to be in His will.

I am worthy, I am anointed, I am powerful, I am blessed, and I walk in God's favor.

In the name of Jesus Christ, this is my declaration.

Notes....

43
NEW CREATION

There is one so perfect and righteous full of virtue and we must strive to becoming more like Him, Christ our Lord and Savior. To become hearers and doers of the word of God and we must leave sinful thoughts and ways. Romans 12:2 (KJV) Be not conformed to this world; but be ye transformed by the renewing of your mind that ye may prove what is that good, and acceptable and perfect will of God.

I declare that He must increase but I must decrease. He that cometh from above is above all. (John 3:30-31, KJV)

I declare by the mercies of God to present my body a living sacrifice, holy, acceptable unto God, which is my reasonable service. (Romans 12:1, KJV)

I declare to be renewed in the spirit of my mind and to put on a new man, which after God is created in righteousness and true holiness. (Ephesians 4:23-24, KJV)

I declare that I have become a new creature in Christ Jesus where the old things have passed away and all things are become new. (2 Corinthians 5:17, KJV)

I declare that I walk in love as Christ had loved us and hath given Himself for us an offering and a sacrifice to God for a sweet-smelling savor. (Ephesians 5:2, KJV)

He who died and rose and yet still lives, Our Lord and Savior Jesus Christ, this is my declaration.

Notes....

44

GO IN SECRET

God's will above and below, He sustains our day, forgives us as we forgive others, with temptation avoided, wrongdoing dismissed from the thought, for His is the kingdom, the power, and the glory. In Jesus's name Amen.

I declare when I fast, to anoint my head, and wash my face so that man will not know, but unto the Father in secret.
(Matthew 6:18, KJV)

I declare when I pray not to be of vain repetitions as the heathen.
(Matthew 6:7, KJV)

I declare when I pray, to go into my closet, shut the door and pray to the Father in secret. (Matthew 6:6, KJV)

I declare to use the "Our Father Prayer" as my guide according to the word of Jesus.

I declare that all things whatsoever I ask in prayer I believe I have received.

Jesus said, "If ye abide in me, and my words abide in you, you shall ask what you will, and it shall be done unto you." (John 15:7, KJV)

This is my declaration.

Notes....

45
FAITH

A man wholeheartedly and completely convicted with God and His word, was Noah who received God's grace, and his family was saved from the destruction of everything else he and his family knew. Because Noah had faith. Ephesians 2:8-9 (KJV) For by grace are ye saved through faith; and that not of yourselves; it is the gift of God: Not of works, lest any man should boast.

I declare without faith it is impossible to please God.

I declare faith cometh by hearing and hearing by the word of God.

I declare I am not ashamed of the gospel of Christ for therein the righteousness of God is revealed from faith to faith: as it is written the just shall live by faith. (Romans 1:17, KJV)

I declare to fight the good fight of faith, to lay hold on eternal life, to which I was also called. (1 Timothy 6:12, KJV)

I declare I am not ashamed of the gospel of Christ for therein the righteousness of God is revealed from faith to faith: as it is written the just shall live by faith. (Romans 1:17, KJV)

In Matthew 17:20, KJV, Jesus said, "If you have faith as a grain of a mustard seed you shall say to this mountain remove, hence to yonder and it shall remove. And nothing shall be impossible unto you."

This is my declaration.

Notes....

46

IN MY OBEDIENCE

The mighty God we serve blesses us for our faithfulness, obedience, truth, right standing, devotion, and honor for an awe-inspiring God. Of Him some claim to be but fail in their deliverance of their word. There is only one true God, creator, not even a man that He should lie. His word is the same today, yesterday, and forever more. Deuteronomy 8:18, But thou shalt remember the Lord thy God; for it is He that giveth thee power to get wealth, that He may establish His covenant.

I declare I am the head, not the tail; I am above and not beneath. I am the lender and not the borrower. (Deuteronomy 28:13, KJV)

I declare to pay my tithes; God will open up windows of Heaven and pour me out blessings I don't have room to receive.
(Malachi 3:10, KJV)

I declare to let not the amount of my giving be known to man, for God sees in secret and will reward openly. (Matthew 6:4, KJV)

I declare to store my treasures in Heaven where they will be eternal where neither moth nor rust corrupt nor thieves steal.
(Matthew 6:20, KJV)

I declare to be faithful and honest that I may abound in blessings.
(Proverbs 28:20, KJV)

I declare to be a good man to leave an inheritance to my children's children. (Proverbs 13:22, KJV)

Because of grace our Lord Jesus Christ, even though He was rich, became poor that through His poverty, we might become rich and, in His virtue, this is my declaration.

Notes....

47

GOD GIVEN PURPOSE

God called Moses unto Mount Sinai, when Moses returned, he had to cover his face with a veil so that his brother and the children of Israel would not be afraid, because Moses' face shone from the glory of God. (Exodus 34:30, KJV) But our faith in Christ Jesus our Lord allows us behind the veil, into the glory of our heavenly Father.

I declare that I seek those things which are above where Christ is seated on the right hand of God. (Colossians 3:1, KJV)

I declare to set my affections on things above not on this earth. (Colossians 3:2, KJV)

I declare to be in the Lord, for He is the Spirit and where the Spirit is there is liberty. (2 Corinthians 3:17, KJV)

I declare thy kingdom come. Thy will be done in earth, as it is in heaven. (Matthew 6:10, KJV)

I declare a new, bolder better me that walks in my God given purpose.

In the name of God, the Father, The Son, and the Holy Spirit, this is my declaration.

Notes....

48

AGAPE

God the Father: What greater world than that which He created? What greater love than what He shows? What greater sacrifice than that which He gave? What greater life than that of everlasting peace?

I declare that I put on a new man, which is renewed in knowledge after the image of He who created Him. (Colossians 3:10, KJV)

I declare to be as the Son who came to seek and save that which is lost. (Luke 19:10, KJV)

I declare to be swift to hear, slow to speak and slow to wrath. (James 1:19, KJV)

I declare to die to sin, to live to righteousness. (1 Peter 2:24, KJV)

I declare to be changed into the same image from glory to glory, even as by the Spirit of the Lord. (2 Corinthians 3:18, KJV)

Our bread and water, cornerstone, counselor, high tower, fortress, Lord and master of our lives, Jesus Christ, this is my declaration.

Notes....

49
SUFFICIENT IN TODAY

Wondering about endlessly with a mind cluttered and confused. Worried about tomorrow when today has enough worry in itself. Now, free your mind and your heart to the love and peace of God. Surrendering to His will.

I declare I rejoice in hope, patient in tribulation and steadfast in prayer (Romans 12:12, KJV)

I declare I am the salt of the earth and the light of the world (Matthew 5:13-14, KJV)

I declare blessed are my eyes, for they see, and my ears for they hear. (Matthew 13:16, KJV)

I declare to refrain my tongue from evil, and my lips that they speak no guile. (1 Peter 2:10, KJV)

I declare not to harden my heart from the voice of the Lord. (Hebrews 3:8, KJV)

Blessed be to God who first loved us, in the name of His son, Jesus.

This is my declaration.

Notes....

50

TREASURED

Why spend your days filled with disappearing benefits of the hopeless heart? When treasures are to be stored above where they neither rot nor be eaten by moths. Fill your heart with eternal blessings that are in the hope of the Lord.

I declare it is God who worketh in me to will and do of his good pleasure. (Philippians 2:13, KJV)

I declare all things work together for the good of them that love God. (Romans 8:28, KJV)

I declare to be steadfast, unmovable, always abounding in the work of the Lord, I know it is not in vain. (1 Corinthians 15:58, KJV)

I declare to work heartily unto the Lord and not man, because unto the Lord, I receive the reward of the inheritance.
(Colossians 3:23-24, KJV)

I declare the beauty of the Lord our God be upon me and establish the work of my hands. (Psalms 90:17, KJV)

Jesus, I give you the honor because without you I can do nothing, this is my declaration.

Notes....

51

STAND

Prosperous Disciples! We must refuse to be overthrown in the wilderness and to wonder about for forty years. We hearken and humble ourselves to the word of the Lord. It is there that we learn to quiet the storm. We were created to win.

I declare blessed are my eyes, for they see, and my ears for they hear. (Matthew 13:16, KJV)

I declare because of Jesus Christ; I received an abundance of grace and the gift of righteousness and I reign in life. (Romans 5:17, KJV)

I declare to study and show myself approved unto God, I am not ashamed, rightly dividing the word of truth. (2 Timothy 2:15, KJV)

I declare to receive the wisdom of God, out of His mouth comes knowledge and understanding. (Proverbs 2:6, KJV)

I declare to walk by faith and not by sight, I am confident and willing to be absent from the body and present with the Lord. (2 Corinthians 5:7-8, KJV)

In the name of He who freely justified me through His redemption, this is my declaration.

Notes....

52

SEEK HIS FACE

I am a child of God, given to earthly parents, yet God knew me before they bore me. He knows I was a sinner; yet because of His agape love, He calls me His own. And my mind will forever be stayed on Him, and one day I shall hear Him say, well done my good and faithful servant.

I declare for all the people to praise the Lord; His merciful kindness is great toward us. (Psalms 117, KJV)

I declare gladness as we go into the house of the Lord: for we are not to forsake the assembling of ourselves together.
(Hebrews 10:25, KJV)

I declare that I believe, and I worship God in spirit and in truth.
(John 4:24, KJV)

I declare that I overcome so that Jesus may grant that I sit with Him in His throne. (Revelation 3:22, KJV)

I declare to the only wise God our Savior, be glory and majesty, dominion, and power, now and forever. (Jude 25, KJV)

My life is now hidden with Christ in God, this is my declaration.

Epilogue

Here I am Lord, use me to bless someone today. This world has never been about you or me. It has always been about God and His will, His way. However, please know this, that we stand behind a giant. And I am not speaking of His size; I am talking about the POWER that is in His name. "Jesus" Son of the living God, our Father in Heaven. And we can stand because of the victory of the power behind that name that overcame this world "Jesus." And yet, we fight the enemy eye to eye as if it has the power in which we possess. Let the enemy know that you know it has already been defeated. We must stop allowing strongholds of the enemy. Trust God's Holy Spirit and discern your steppingstones, move past the emotions that are only there to stagnate you. This is the cry of the righteous word. Fearless warriors rise! God has blessed us with all authority to take captive the naysayers and become the heads we were created to be. Obedience has been taught, tried, and accomplished. Walls of distraction, I command you to come down! And I release focus. Spirits of bondage release God's people, I bind you to the pits of darkness. And I loose freedom to work in God's word.

We are no longer slaves to evil and no more servants of sin. We are under God given authority. For we all want to hear, "well done my good and faithful servant," then now is the time to stand. Let this book be your beginning, for in the beginning was the word. And the word was made flesh. That means God's word is alive, use it for your purpose given life. Rise up confident warrior. Speak to God and tell God, here I am Lord, use me to bless someone today.

May God's word pierce the soul vibrate the flesh and ignite the faith; may our belief stand in the boldness God placed inside of us all. For the Little children who cry themselves to sleep at night because they do not understand what's going on in this world, comfort them with the song of David 2 Samuel 22, and to the ones who walk in shame and hold back tears whose pride keeps them from reaching for a helping hand, let God use you as a ministering disciple with words of encouragement that leads them to His light. Rise faithful warrior and say, "Here I am Lord, use me to bless someone today."

This is the time where self can be no more, and the purpose God has placed in us stand at all times. Kingdom builders allow yourselves to be uncomfortable if it is necessary to achieve the work of His way, be an outcast if you must, just be consistent with His will. Be always on fire for God, finding the peace of Him that eliminates any doubt and any fear. Be bold in your God given authority, tell that mountain my God is bigger, quiet the storm, say as Jesus said, peace be still, command the atmospheres to shift for God is here! Walk in dominion for we house the spirit of the Lord! Here I am Lord use me to bless someone today. Command this time, this new year is our time. Walk in assurance because you know God's word is so.

When God knocks, answer, When God speaks listen. Act immediately upon His instruction, because the door to your assignment is open, if you prolong your reaction or your response, it may not be as easy to walk through. And let your request to Him be known through prayer and supplication with thanksgiving as He says. For the simplicity of the ask is in His son Jesus's name, just make sure you are not walking contrary to His word. And then you wonder why your prayer was not answered with the "right now" faith you placed on it. God's will for our lives can no longer be suppressed. Proverbs 28 says, the wicked flee when no man pursueth but the righteous are bold as a lion. And we are righteous through Christ Jesus. Here I am Lord, use me to bless someone today. Ephesians says in whom we have boldness and access with confidence through faith in him. Holy Holy Holy Lord God Almighty which was and is and is to come.

INDEX

1. Have Faith   11
2. Choose God   13
3. Sin no More   15
4. Stay Ready for War   17
5. Praise Him   19
6. Do you Believe?   21
7. Continue to Climb   23
8. Because He is   25
9. He in Me   27
10. Let God be the Guide   29
11. Who I Am   31
12. My Assignment   33
13. Hope   35
14. Provider   37
15. Jesus   39
16. Because of Him   41
17. Unlike You or Me   43
18. The Fruit   45
19. I in Him   47
20. Grace   49
21. His Mercy   51
22. Forgive your Enemy   53
23. Unlimited Goodness   55
24. Fearful, yet Strong   57
25. Cleansed   59
26. The Cross   61
27. God Multiplies   63
28. Be Zealous   65
29. God's Timing   67
30. Love   69
31. He Calls me His Own   71
32. Pray the Word   73
33. Called to Be   75
34. Let go and Let God   77
35. Seek His Face   79
36. It is Already Done   81
37. Understanding   83
38. Close but no Harm   85
39. Before creation   87
40. Just Believe   89
41. God   91
42. I will I Am   93
43. New Creation   95
44. Go in Secret   97
45. Faith   99
46. In my Obedience   101
47. God Given   105
48. Agape   107
49. Sufficient in Today   109
50. Treasured   111
51. Stand   113
52. Seek His face   115